Alternator Books™

INDIGENOUS CULTURES TODAY

Protecting Native Families and Practicing Cultural Traditions

CAYLA BELLANGER DEGROAT

Lerner Publications ◆ Minneapolis

To Bizaan and Mitig

Content consultant: Jill Doerfler

Copyright © 2025 by Lerner Publishing Group, Inc.

All rights reserved. International copyright secured. No part of this book may be reproduced, stored in a retrieval system, or transmitted in any form or by any means—electronic, mechanical, photocopying, recording, or otherwise—without the prior written permission of Lerner Publishing Group, Inc., except for the inclusion of brief quotations in an acknowledged review.

Lerner Publications Company
An imprint of Lerner Publishing Group, Inc.
241 First Avenue North
Minneapolis, MN 55401 USA

For reading levels and more information, look up this title at www.lernerbooks.com.

Main body text set in Aptifer Sans LT Pro Medium.
Typeface provided by Linotype AG.

Designer: Athena Currier

Map illustration on page 28 by Laura K. Westlund

Library of Congress Cataloging-in-Publication Data

Names: DeGroat, Cayla Bellanger, author.
Title: Indigenous cultures today : protecting Native families and practicing cultural traditions / Cayla Bellanger DeGroat.
Other titles: Protecting Native families and practicing cultural traditions
Description: Minneapolis : Lerner Publications, [2025]. | Series: Native rights (Alternator Books) | Includes bibliographical references and index. | Audience: Ages 8–12 | Audience: Grades 4–6 | Summary: "Indigenous peoples are proudly reclaiming their cultures. Young readers discover how boarding schools took Native peoples away from their families and cultures. They also learn how Indigenous peoples are protecting their languages and traditions today"— Provided by publisher
Identifiers: LCCN 2023040539 (print) | LCCN 2023040540 (ebook) | ISBN 9798765625576 (lib. bdg.) | ISBN 9798765629147 (pbk.) | ISBN 9798765635889 (epub)
Subjects: LCSH: Indians of North America—Ethnic identity—Juvenile literature. | Cultural rights—United States—Juvenile literature. | Indians of North America—Social life and customs—Juvenile literature.
Classification: LCC E98.E85 D44 2025 (print) | LCC E98.E85 (ebook) | DDC 305.897–dc23/eng/20231108

LC record available at https://lccn.loc.gov/2023040539
LC ebook record available at https://lccn.loc.gov/2023040540

Manufactured in the United States of America
2-1012563-51891-4/10/2025

TABLE OF CONTENTS

INTRODUCTION Protecting Native Children 4

CHAPTER 1 Education and Family Systems 6

CHAPTER 2 Boarding Schools and Assimilation 10

CHAPTER 3 Indian Child Welfare Act 19

CHAPTER 4 Restoring Indigenous Languages and Cultures 25

    Glossary 30
    Learn More 31
    Index 32

INTRODUCTION
PROTECTING NATIVE CHILDREN

On June 15, 2023, advocates for Native American rights and tribal Nations celebrated a victory. The Supreme Court of the United States decided to uphold, or continue to support, the Indian Child Welfare Act (ICWA). ICWA is an important law that keeps Native American children in the foster care system with Native American families.

Native American advocates and activists worried that the Supreme Court would rule against them. If that happened, Native children could have been taken away from their nations and separated from their families and communities. The US government had taken Native children away from their loved ones before. But Native American peoples have always shown great strength and courage when it comes to protecting their children and loved ones.

A citizen (*right*) of the Alabama-Coushatta Tribe of Texas celebrates the Supreme Court's decision to uphold the ICWA with a hug.

CHAPTER 1
Education and Family Systems

What makes a family? There are many different types of families across the world and across different groups of people. For Native American peoples, family is a large network of people you care about and who care about you. They may or may not be related. Either way they support one another.

Clan System

Many Native American tribes organized their societies by clan. Clan systems are family groups that people in a community may share. For many tribes, such as the Ojibwe, each clan had certain duties and responsibilities. In Haudenosaunee society, women were the heads of their families and clans. They also helped lead their tribe. Clans are still important in many tribes today.

A Shoshone-Bannock elder reads to children.

wakanyeja

In many Native American cultures, children are precious. The Lakota word for child, wakanyeja, means sacred being. Children are also important to their communities and Nations because they will one day become the leaders. Native American tribes recognize that without children, they have no future.

REFLECT

Think about people who support you in your life. How is this similar to or different from the ways peoples in Native Nations support one another?

Taos Pueblo citizens shuck corn.

Before boarding schools, people in the tribes taught and cared for the children. It wasn't just the parents' job to raise them. The children learned lessons from all the adults. They spent their days with immediate and extended family as they prepared food, tended crops, gathered food and medicines, and more. Children watched closely, and then tried their own hand at doing the work. This is how they learned to be good community members and care for their families.

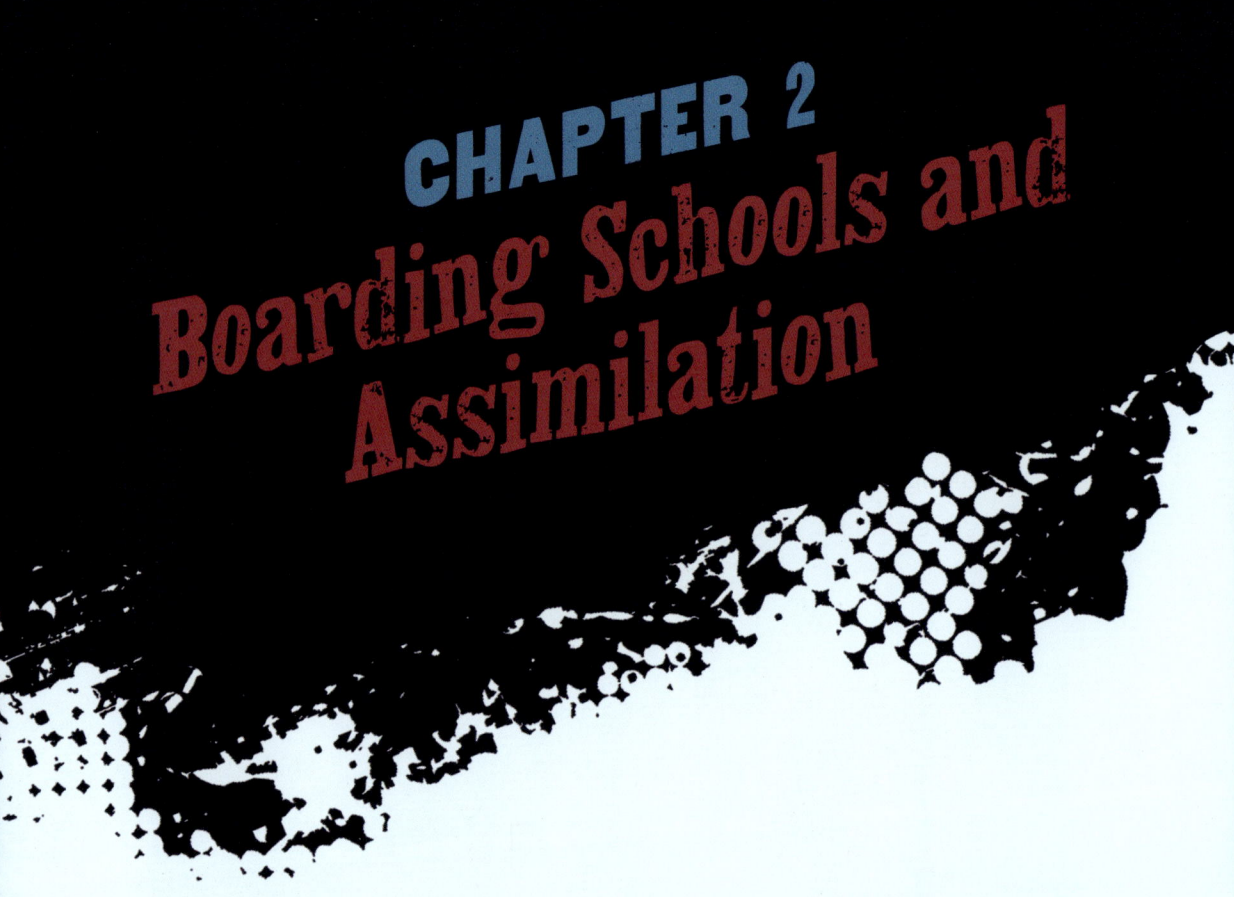

CHAPTER 2
Boarding Schools and Assimilation

Family life for Native American children changed in the late 1800s. From then to the 1970s, Christian missionaries and the US government began forcing them to attend boarding schools. Children were sent away from their families to schools that were sometimes hundreds of miles away from their homes. Boarding schools tried to force Native American children to assimilate. This meant taking on the values, beliefs, and behaviors of white people.

The US and Boarding Schools

During this time, white men controlled the US government. They judged others who lived differently from them. They wrongly thought that people from different races and cultures would be better off if they were more like white people.

Taking kids from Native Nations also made it easier for the US government to take their land. Nations wouldn't have a future without their children. Their population size would grow smaller. Their nations would not have people to carry it on.

Sioux children at the Carlisle Indian Industrial School

Children and Their Cultures

At boarding schools, children weren't allowed to speak in their Native languages and had to speak English. The schools changed the kids' names to English ones. The students were not allowed to practice the spiritual teachings their families passed onto them. The students had to convert to Christianity and live like white Christians.

REFLECT

Do you feel safe and welcome at your school? If not, who can you talk to about it? How can you help make your school more welcoming for your classmates?

Native American children forced to do physical labor at a boarding school in 1935

Native children were punished for their cultures and being themselves. Boarding schools did not care for Native children. Many children were not fed enough. They were also often physically and sexually abused by the people who worked there. Some did not receive medical treatment when they were sick. Thousands of kids died at boarding schools and the schools didn't always tell their parents.

Until the 1940s, children usually spent only a couple hours in the classroom learning subjects such as math and reading. Most of the students' days were spent working. Some worked for white families by sewing and cooking. Others worked on the school farm raising livestock and growing food for the school. Many also chopped wood, made bricks, and built railroads.

BOARDING SCHOOL INITIATIVE

Native nations are healing from boarding schools. But the US government has been slow to recognize the pain they caused at boarding schools. In 2021, Secretary of the Interior Deb Haaland announced the Federal Indian Boarding School Initiative. It will look into the harm that happened at the boarding schools. It will look for unmarked graves of students who died at the schools and make sure their stories are told.

Secretary Haaland is the first Native American cabinet secretary.

A mother and daughter of the Hopi Nation stand together.

Taking a Stand

As early as the 1910s, former students and others spoke out against the abuse of boarding schools. Native American families also pushed back. Some parents ran away with their children before they could be taken away. Some children ran away from the schools to return to their nations, though many didn't make it.

In 2022, a Standing Rock Sioux citizen speaks about her experience at a boarding school.

While in boarding schools, some children kept a connection to their tribes by secretly speaking their languages. Some students used an Indigenous sign language to communicate with their classmates.

Many boarding school survivors are still making sense of what happened at the schools. They may have been abused or forced to give up parts of their identities. They might not remember cultural practices or their Native language. This has also affected their children and future generations. The number of Native language speakers has declined.

SOCIETY OF AMERICAN INDIANS

In 1911, fifty Native people from several nations came together. They created the Society of American Indians. It was the first Indigenous rights group created by and for Native peoples. They spoke up about the challenges they faced and criticized the US government. They lobbied in Congress and got some changes made.

People gather for the Society of American Indians' conference in 1915.

Today many Native American languages have very small numbers of speakers, but beginning in the 1970s many Native nations started language programs so that more people could learn their language. The last boarding schools finally closed in the 1970s. By then the US government had a new way to force assimilation.

Citizens of Ketchikan Indian Community learn the Tsimshian language, Shm'algyack.

CHAPTER 3
Indian Child Welfare Act

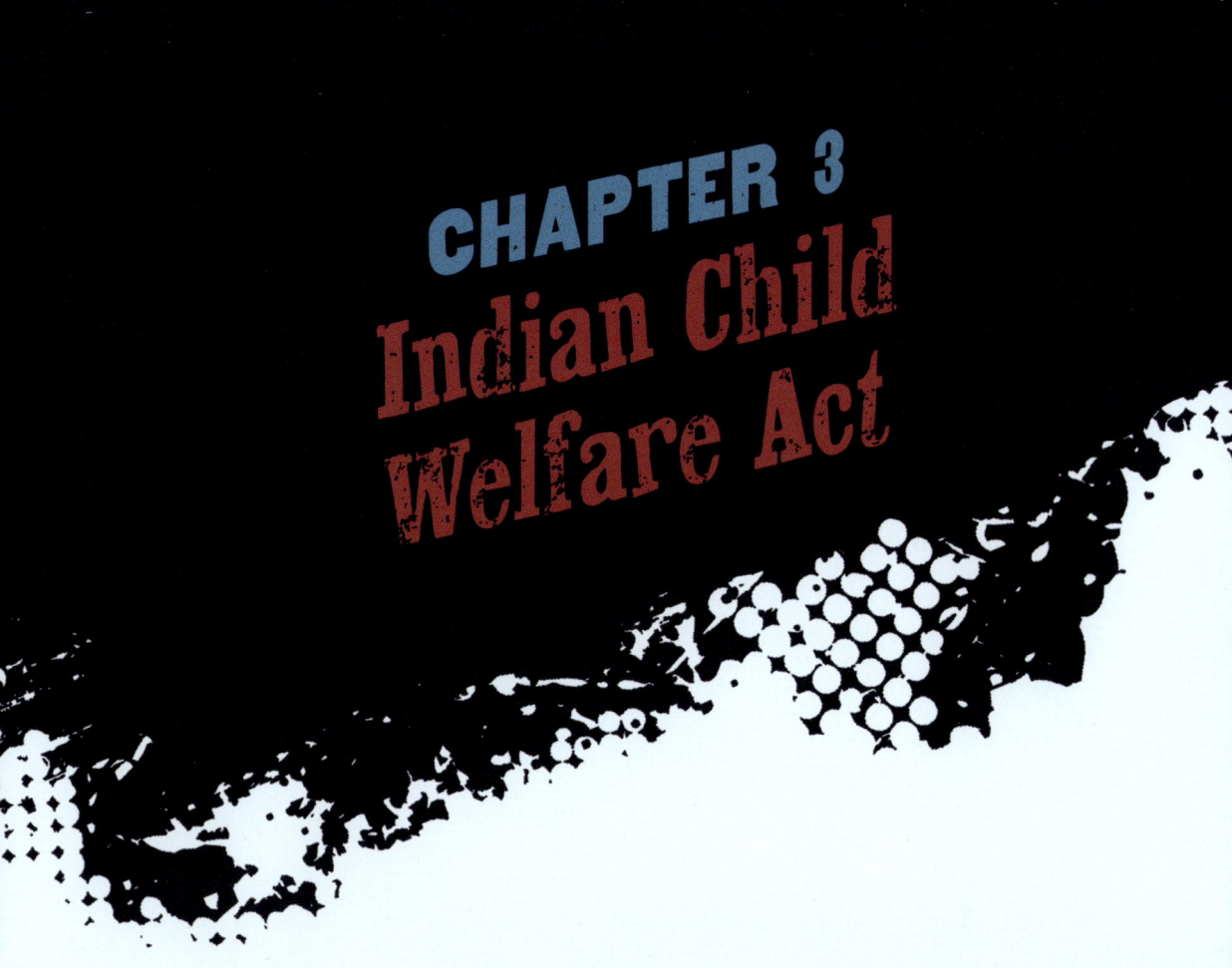

By the 1950s and 1960s most Native American children attended local public schools, but there was a new threat to Native families. US agencies began taking Native American children away from their families. Many children were taken as newborn babies. Most of the kids had loving families and were not in any danger at home but social workers thought the children would have a better life with a white family.

Adoption

They were often taken because social service agencies held racist beliefs against Native American mothers and families. In 1978, 35 percent of all Native American kids were taken from their homes. Most were adopted by white families.

Adopted children often found it difficult or impossible to find their birth families because records were kept secret. They couldn't learn about where they came from. They couldn't connect with their nation to learn cultural traditions. The children weren't able to pass on these practices to future generations.

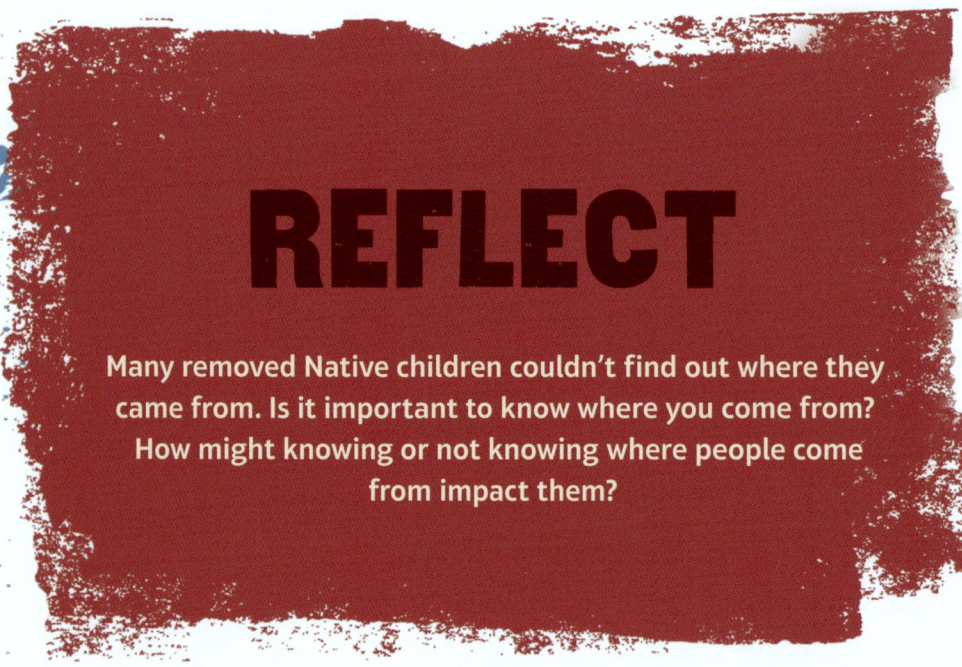

REFLECT

Many removed Native children couldn't find out where they came from. Is it important to know where you come from? How might knowing or not knowing where people come from impact them?

Native American peoples celebrate their cultures in 1986.

Supporting Children

In the 1970s more Native peoples spoke out against these removals. An Indigenous organization called Association on American Indian Affairs worked to protect the sovereignty of Native Nations. They gathered data about the removal of Native American children. Then they lobbied for a law that protected Native American children from unfair removal from their homes.

In 1978, ICWA was passed. The act helps stop children from being taken from their homes and adopted by other families. Many people worked hard for years to help pass ICWA.

ICWA

With ICWA, Native nations decide what happens to children living in unsafe homes. Tribes are sovereign nations, or independent countries, so they have their own child protection laws, courts, and staff. They know how to handle childcare cases.

If children aren't in a safe home, ICWA has rules about where they should go. Preference is given to foster homes of the same nation, another family member, or a Native American household. Also, the child's tribe must be told where they are going. Then tribal social services can help the child to make sure they are safe. They can also help the child return to their home if it becomes safe.

REFLECT

What are some traditions your family or culture have passed on to you? How do these traditions teach you about who you are as a person?

Citizens of Pascua Yaqui, who were protected by ICWA

ICWA helps Native American kids keep their culture. They can attend ceremonies and meet with people in their community. This makes tribes stronger and more connected.

Jingle dancers perform at the 2019 Mille Lacs Band of Ojibwe Grand Celebration Powwow.

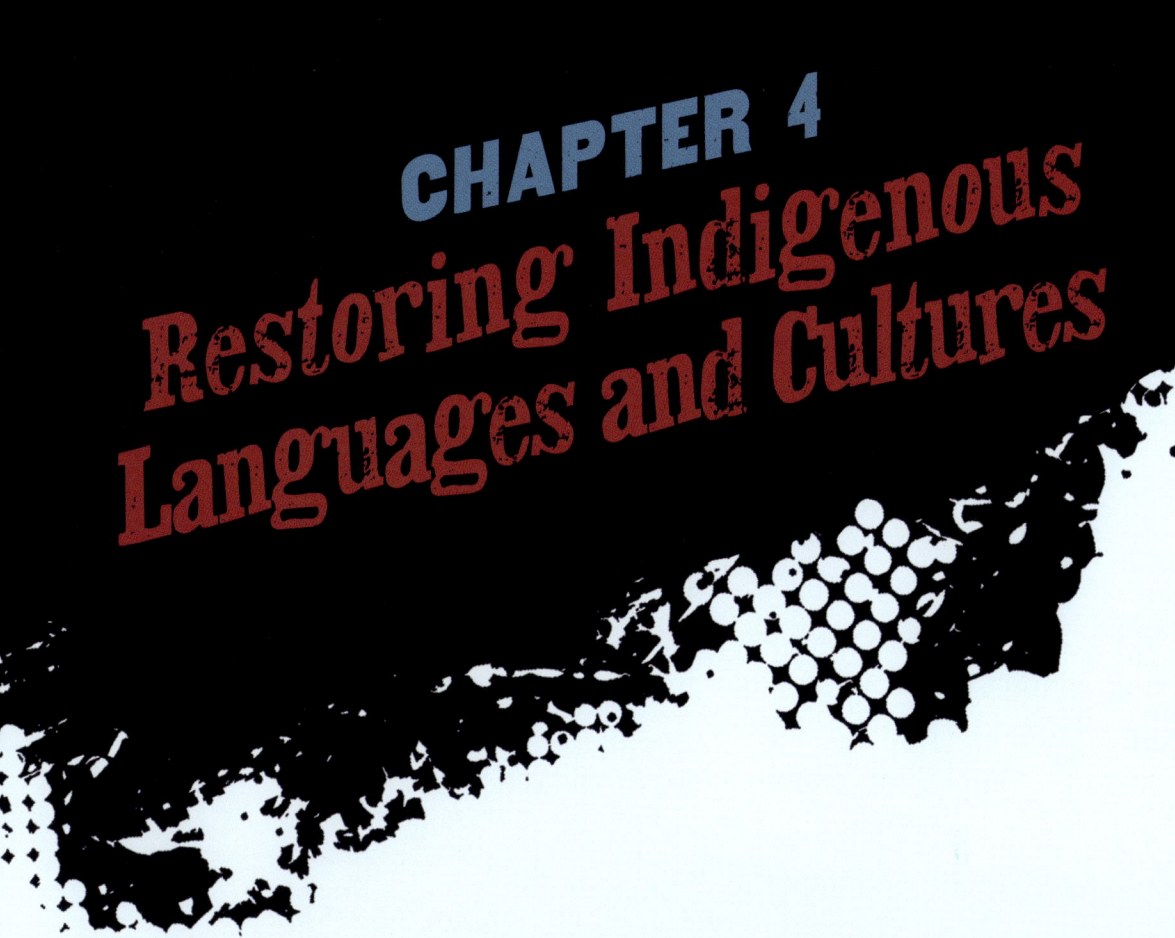

CHAPTER 4
Restoring Indigenous Languages and Cultures

Many Native American peoples are rediscovering the joy in their cultures and languages. They are learning and speaking their Indigenous languages. They are also bringing back cultural practices. They are connecting with the teachings of their ancestors and bringing this wisdom into the future of their nations.

Beliefs

In 1978 the American Indian Religious Freedom Act passed. This allowed Native American peoples to practice their traditional spiritual beliefs legally. Before, it was illegal for Native Americans to have their spiritual objects or perform traditional religious ceremonies. People could have been fined or imprisoned for their religion.

Languages

Language revitalization is bringing back Indigenous languages. Revitalizing a language means increasing the use of a language that is rarely used. Some nations are bringing back their languages by teaching them in schools and tribal programs.

The Mille Lacs Band of Ojibwe worked with a software company to create a computer and cell phone app that

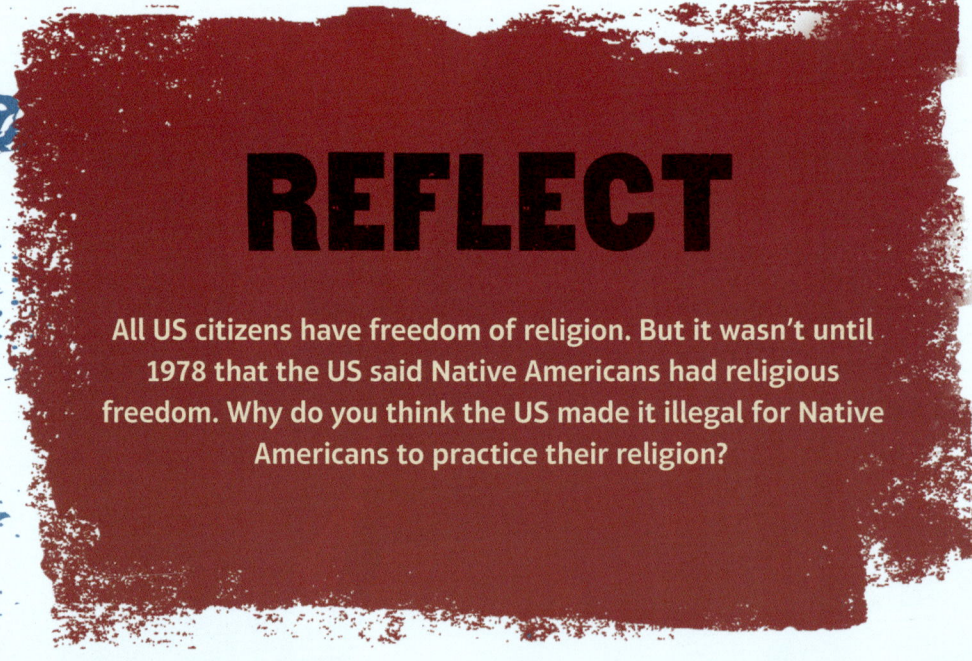

REFLECT

All US citizens have freedom of religion. But it wasn't until 1978 that the US said Native Americans had religious freedom. Why do you think the US made it illegal for Native Americans to practice their religion?

A citizen of the Odawa Indians writes in Anishinaabemowin.

helps people learn the Ojibwe language, Ojibwemowin. The Navajo Nation's native speakers also translated popular movies into the Navajo language. These programs give students of all ages access to their Indigenous languages and tools to become better speakers. Indigenous languages strengthen Native peoples' connection to their culture and spiritual practices.

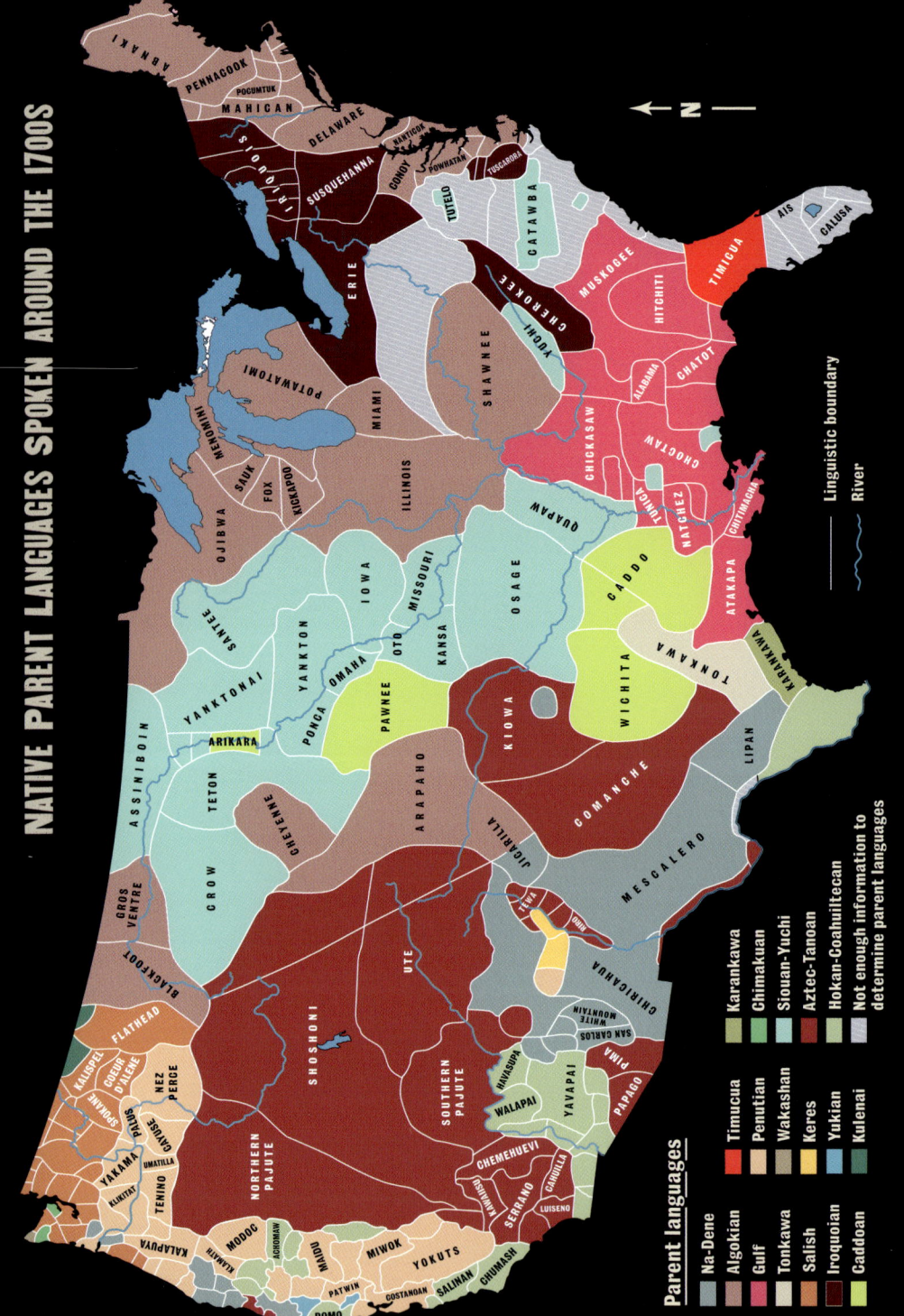

Indigenous children celebrating their culture

Native American peoples are reclaiming their cultures and languages. They are embracing traditions that were denied to many ancestors and elders through boarding schools and adoptions. Modern Native American cultures and expressions continue to grow in people's daily lives through art and more. Indigenous peoples are bringing their cultures and Nations into the future.

Glossary

assimilation: the process whereby individuals or groups of differing ethnic heritage are absorbed into the dominant culture of a society

clan: a kin group used as an organizational device in many traditional societies

racist: someone or something that assumes that members of racial categories have distinctive characteristics and that these differences result in some racial groups being inferior to others

revitalization: the process of giving something a new life or making it healthy

sacred: considered to be holy and deserving of respect

sovereignty: the power that a nation has to govern itself

Supreme Court: the highest court of law in some countries including the US

translate: to change words from one language into another

Learn More

Bellanger DeGroat, Cayla. *Native Voting Rights and Sovereignty: Recognizing Indigenous Voices in Government*. Minneapolis: Lerner Publications, 2025.

Britannica Kids: Indigenous Peoples of the Americas
https://kids.britannica.com/kids/article/Indigenous-Peoples-of-the-Americas/353288

Britannica Kids: Native Boarding Schools
https://kids.britannica.com/kids/article/Native-boarding-schools/635496

Doerfler, Jill, and Matthew J. Martinez. *Deb Haaland: First Native American Cabinet Secretary*. Minneapolis: Lerner Publications, 2023.

James, Trisha. *Native American Art*. New York: Cavendish Square, 2023.

National Geographic Kids: Native Americans
https://kids.nationalgeographic.com/history/topic/native-americans

Native Languages: Native American Facts for Kids
https://www.native-languages.org/kids.htm

Washburne, Sophie. *The Story of the Native American Rights Movement*. Buffalo, NY: Cavendish Square, 2024.

Index

American Indian Religious Freedom Act, 25

Association on American Indian Affairs, 21

boarding schools, 9–10, 12–16, 18, 29

Haaland, Deb, 14

Indian Child Welfare Act (ICWA), 4, 21–22, 24

language revitalization, 26

Mille Lacs Band of Ojibwe, 26

Navajo Nation, 27

Ojibwemowin, 27

Society of American Indians, 17

wakanyeja, 8

Photo Acknowledgments

Images: Minh Connors/The Washington Post/Getty Images, p. 5; Angel Wynn/DanitaDelimont.com/Alamy, p. 7; John Cancalosi/Alamy, p. 9; Library of Congress, p. 11; Keystone View Company/FPG/Archive Photos/Getty Images, p. 13; Shannon Finney/Getty Images, p. 14; Keystone-Burton Holmes/FPG/Archive Photos/Hulton Archive/Getty Images, p. 15; AP Photo/Sue Ogrocki, p. 16; Courtesy of the University of Kansas Libraries, p. 17; AP Photo/Taylor Balkom/Ketchikan Daily News, p. 18; AP Photo/Joan Sonapley, p. 21; Joshua Lott/The Washington Post/Getty Images, p. 23; AP Photo/Photographer, p. 24; AP Photo/Petoskey News-Review, Christina Rohn, p. 27; Laura K. Westlund/Independent Picture Service, p. 28; Sylvain GRANDADAM/Gamma-Rapho/Getty Images, p. 29. Design elements: Kiwihug/Unsplash; mikesj11/Shutterstock; Forgem/Shutterstock; galacticus/Shutterstock; Archiwiz/Shutterstock; Miloje/Shutterstock.

Cover: aarrows/Shutterstock; NadzeyaShanchuk/Shutterstock.